WE LOVE A CHALLENGE!

BLOOMSBURY EDUCATION

Bloomsbury Publishing Plc
50 Bedford Square, London WC1B 3DP, UK

Bloomsbury Publishing Ireland Limited
29 Earlsfort Terrace, Dublin 2, D02 AY28, Ireland

First published in Great Britain, 2026 by Bloomsbury Publishing Plc

A catalogue record for this book is available from the British Library

ISBN: PB: 9-781-80199-810-9; ePub: 9-781-80199-809-3

2 4 6 8 10 9 7 5 3 1

Printed and bound in China by C&C Offset Printing Co., Ltd., Shenzhen, Guangdong

WE LOVE A CHALLENGE!

BLOOMSBURY EDUCATION
LONDON OXFORD NEW YORK NEW DELHI SYDNEY

From Dubai to Darjeeling,
from Lima to Loch Ness,
you'll hear this first reaction...

Do you know it?

Can you guess?

It comes at the start of a challenge
when you're facing something new,
that feels too big, too tricky, too tough
for you to see it through...

Ali the African Land Snail
was dreaming of winning a race.
But what chance did he have with one slimy foot?
'There's no way I could ever keep pace...'

START
12
08
02

Louis the Lion had a secret...
He was longing to learn how to swim.
But he worried that he might look silly
and the others would all laugh at him.

Mimi the Monkey was staring
at the vine across the river.
'That's bananas!' she gulped, **'I can't jump that far!'**
as her legs began to quiver...

Willow the Warthog was hoping
to sing like a jungle pop star.
'But what if I sound like a buffalo's burp?
It's **HOPELESS**, I'll never go far!'
It's too hard!

The animals had almost decided
giving up was the best thing to do,
when a **RUMBLE** grew out of the jungle...
and a voice **YELLING**...

Poo coming through!

'Hey dudes!' buzzed Larry the Dung Beetle
as he parked his ball under a tree.
'You seem a bit sad, what's the challenge my friends?
We'll solve this together, you'll see!'

The animals each shared their struggles
and Larry listened a while.
Then he turned with his eyes full of kindness
and held out his claws with a smile.

‘I know what it’s like to feel hopeless,
when the road up ahead looks rough.
And all those negative thoughts kick in,
“Quit now! You’re not strong enough!”’

'My friends, let me tell you a **SECRET**
that a wise mouse once shared with me.
Whenever you're facing a challenge
just plant your feet strong like a tree!'

‘Turn to that challenge and tell it:
“You look tough but I won’t run away!”
Smile and look at it right in the face,
then rub your hands together and say...

"I LOVE A CHALLENGE!"

‘It's best to start with small steps
and ask for the help that you need.
It takes tumbles and stumbles and slip-ups
but keep trying and soon you’ll succeed.’

The friends glanced around at each other,
could their challenges really be fun?
No need to be perfect, just give it a try,
then grow with each step, one by one.

Ali slid up to the start line,
'I might not come first, but that's still great.'

'I do love a challenge', he yelled coming last.
'When's the next race? I can't wait!'

Louis dipped his toe in the water,
then let out a terrified squeak!
But with lots of practice and help from a friend
he really improved his technique.

Mimi signed up to a sports club

training hard, round the clock, day and night.

Each leap got her closer and closer...

...till she swung from the vine with delight.

I love, love,
love a challenge!

Willow edged into the spotlight,
her ears glowing red at the ends.
It wasn't pitch perfect but everyone cheered
as she sang with some help from her friends.

The animals all came back together
and danced beneath the night sky.

‘You see what can happen, the **power** you have when you **dare** to give hard things a try’.

So next time you're faced with a challenge
that feels too big for you,
remember our friend, little Larry,
and think about what he would do.

Turn to your challenge and tell it:
'You look tough but I won't run away!'
Smile and look at it right in the face,
then rub your hands together and say...

WE LOVE A

CHALLENGE!
08

WELCOME TO...

THE COURAGE CLUB

This story is part of **The Courage Club** series – helping children (and their adults!) build bravery, take risks, and go after hard things together.

The bigger picture

So much of our approach to mental health is reactive: we wait until there's a problem before stepping in to 'fix' it. At *The Courage Club* we believe in a more proactive approach - one that supports ALL children to build strong emotional foundations right from the start. This is not just to equip children with the tools to cope when life's challenges come but also to empower them with the skills to thrive well beyond that.

The Courage Club is built around three core strands of child development:

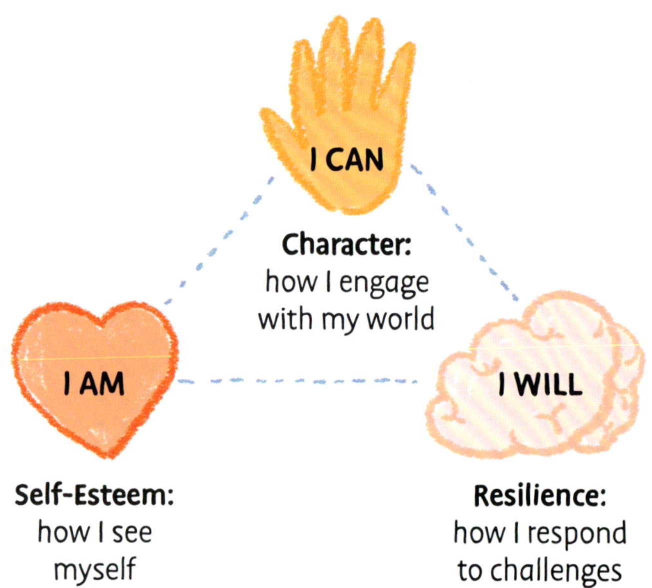

Where this story fits

We Love a Challenge celebrates the joy of tackling something tricky and reminds us that hard things help us grow. When children learn to see challenge as an adventure – something exciting rather than scary – they begin to approach new experiences with curiosity and confidence. Struggle ceases to be a sign of weakness and more a banner of encouragement that we are on the right track.

'Great! This is hard – that means I'm learning!'

When we cheer each other on and share in the fun of figuring things out, we help children discover that effort and the courage to take on hard things is something to be proud of.

So, let's keep saying it out loud, together: